BRIE

The Rim of Fire
Indonesia and the Malay-speaking Muslim world

Glenn Myers

OM publishing

Copyright © 1998 Glenn Myers

First published 1998 by OM Publishing

OM Publishing is an imprint of Paternoster Publishing,
P.O. Box 300, Carlisle, Cumbria, CA3 0QS, U.K.

03 02 01 00 99 98   7 6 5 4 3 2 1

The right of Glenn Myers to be identified as the Author of this Work has been asserted by him in accordance with Copyright, Designs and Patents Act 1988.

All rights reserved. No part of this publication may be reproduced, stored in a retrieval system, or transmitted in any form or by any means, electric, mechanical, photocopying, recording or otherwise, without the prior permission of the publisher or a license permitting restricted copying. In the U.K. such licenses are issued by the Copyright Licensing Agency, 90, Tottenham Court Road, London W1P 9HE.

British Library Cataloguing in Publication Data
A catalogue record for this book is available from the British Library

ISBN 1-85078-298-9

Designed by Christopher Lawther, Teamwork, Lancing, West Sussex.
Typeset by WestKey Ltd, Falmouth, Cornwall.
Produced by Jeremy Mudditt Publishing Services, Carlisle,
and printed and bound in Great Britain by WEC Press, Gerrards Cross, Bucks.

Contents

	Start here	5
1	Indonesia: a necklace of islands	7
2	Beliefs	12
3	How the Church happened	19
4	The far side: where the gospel isn't	28
5	Interesting times	38
6	The challenge for the Church	45
7	Elsewhere on the Rim: the Philippines and Malaysia	53
	Notes	58
	Resources	61
	Praying for the Rim of Fire	64

This book was produced from the International Research and UK Publications departments of WEC International.

WEC International is an interdenominational missions agency aiming to bring the Christian gospel to the remaining unevangelised peoples of the world. WEC has over 1850 workers from 43 nations serving together in 60 countries.

Start here

This booklet looks at Indonesia and then briefly at the other Malay-speaking Muslims who belong to the same great family of peoples as the Indonesians. This great family – as large in population as Western Europe or North America – lives between three great fault lines in the earth's crust, the places where the Eurasian, Indo-Australian and Philippine plates grind against each other. A region of volcanic eruptions and earthquakes, it has been well-named the 'Rim of Fire'.

I took my information from personal interviews with church leaders, missionaries and other expatriates; from the standard sources; and from the unique resources of the WEC International Research Office in the UK. I have checked the quotes and comments back with many of the people whom I interviewed; however, I have preferred usually not to quote them by name in this book.

I hope you'll put up with the generalizations and short-cuts necessary to squeeze useable information into a book this size. I welcome your comments, updates, and corrections.

I would like to thank all the people who worked on this project with me for their kind help. Special thanks to my wife Cordelia and our children.

The photos, except for those on pp 9, 29, 51, 54 and 55, are credited to Roy Spraggett, *One Man's View*, WEC International.

Glenn Myers
Cambridge, 1998.

– 1 –
Indonesia: a necklace of islands

JEWELS

Think of a necklace of islands draped through the shallow tropical waters between Asia and Australia: the Malay Archipalego. It takes five hours to fly from one end to the other, the distance between New York and Los Angeles. History and politics has divided these volcanic islands, and the family of peoples who inhabit them, among several nations: The Philippines, Malaysia, Papua New Guinea, the rich enclaves of Singapore and Brunei – and the regional giant, Indonesia.

Geographers, presumably with a job for life, have mapped more than thirteen thousand islands that make up Indonesia's *tanah air kita* – 'our land and water'. Six thousand of these islands have people on them; these people speak six hundred languages and dialects, more than the United Nations has delegations.

The island of Java is the pendant on the Necklace, Indonesia's centrepiece, with 120m people wedged into a humid, fertile land the size of England or Alabama – twice the size of Tasmania. Like the English in Britain or the white Protestants in the USA, the Javanese set the economic, political, and cultural tone for the whole country.

Strung out either side from Java, and curled back over the top, the Necklace is heavy with jewels. Irian, Kalimantan and Sumatra are three of the world's five biggest islands[1], until recently uncut nuggets of creation. Half of all their flora and fauna is uncharted by science.[2] One in twenty of all the earth's plant species and one in twenty-five of all the terrestrial animal species are probably found on just one of these jungle islands[3].

DEVELOPING FAST

Indonesia is large, and changing fast. Only three nations supply more people to the world than Indonesia (China, India, and the USA): one person in every thirty on earth is Indonesian.

Free from colonial rule since 1945, the country has a familiar tangle of sprouting life and impenetrable problems. Yet economic and material development, and national stability (albeit subject to the odd catastrophe) have been the dominant themes in Indonesia's story.

All the traditional measures of material development have moved impressively in the right direction in the past two generations: Illiteracy rates – for example – have plunged: about 85% of the population can now read.[4] Life expectancy has increased; child health has improved dramatically. Much of the infrastructure for a prosperous nation has been put in place – roads and phone-lines; factories, schools and hospitals; elements of a trained and skilled workforce; a commitment to religious and cultural tolerance – and will not be easily dismantled.

INTERESTING TIMES

Recent problems, of course, have rather overshadowed all this good news. Indonesian soothsayers forecasted that 1998 would be a turbulent year in the nation's history and in ex-president Suharto's personal fortunes. So it proved.

The currency devaluations and stock market collapses that hoovered up much of south east Asia's wealth in 1997 and 1998 savaged the Indonesian economy. Within a few months,[5] Indonesia's currency plunged from perhaps 2,500 to the dollar to 12,000 (17,000 on the day before Suharto resigned), jacking up the cost of imports, putting up to 12m people out of work, and making every bank in the country technically bankrupt.

It was a giant step backwards for Indonesia. It hit the poor especially hard. It felt to some Indonesians that all the careful work of the 32 years of former president Suharto's rule were unpicked in its final calamitous months.

What is left after the meltdown is a nation that could be pulled in any of many directions, or even pulled apart. The famous Chinese curse runs, 'May you live in interesting times'; these years are Indonesia's 'interesting times.'

INDONESIA AND THE CHURCH

The story of Indonesia's Church is also one of great size and rapid development. Millions of Indonesians have joined the Church over the last couple of generations. More people have turned from Islam to Christianity in Indonesia than in any other country. Some of the region's biggest denominations have been born. Revival has flared. Showy miracles have been demonstrated (and also faked).

Yet – as we'll see – growth has been spectacular in some areas and almost invisible in many others.

This booklet looks at:

- How Indonesia has the largest Muslim population in the world, without being a Muslim country at all.

- How many people have turned to Christianity here, and why.

- What's going on in some of South East Asia's biggest churches.

- Which of Indonesia's peoples are least reached by the gospel.

- What the future may hold.
- How Christians can serve this nation.

THE BIG DURIAN

At the economic heart of Java is Indonesia's capital, Jakarta. Its friends call it 'The Durian', after the fat tropical fruit with the heavenly taste and the hellish smell.

Here, about 10m people (5m arriving within the last fifteen years) taste the future of Indonesian development. They enjoy world-class traffic jams. They breathe in an annual ton and a half of lead pollution.[6] Many are looking for work. Some beg aggressively on the streets, pointing to empty stomachs.

They also show the size of the task facing the Christian Church. Indeed, Jakarta could be a test-bed for Christian missions in the new century. If the gospel is up to the challenges here, it can thrive in the post-2000 world:

- Weight of numbers: Shortly into the first decade of the new century, Jakarta will become one of the seven super-cities of the Islamic world as its population zooms past the 10m mark.[7] The city already has more people than most of the countries in the United Nations.

- Poverty: This is the unshakable first impression the visitor gets: a little homeless kid alone in a dark corner, sucking a sweet; a family on the roadside watching the traffic like picnickers on a riverbank while a toddler plays on a flattened cardboard box in the dirt; two street musicians singing on a bus, accompanied by guitar and by a teaspoon scraped rhythmically against a bottle; a barefoot youth siphoning fuel while a tanker waits at a red light, then scampering away through the traffic.

- Pluralism: Jakarta is a city of incompatible beliefs. Mosques (within earshot of everyone) are easier to find than tap water (available to only one Jakarta resident in five). Islam is resurgent, yet Jakarta is also home to more than a thousand Christian churches[8] – proportionately almost as many as neighbouring Singapore. Buddhism and Hinduism have a presence. And for many of the new urban classes, at least until the recent crash, materialism was the grand passion.

- Anger: You can find large areas of Jakarta where in the riots that toppled ex-President Suharto in May 1998 every single shop, bank, restaurant, hotel and place of business was destroyed.[9] Anger at shortages of food overflowed into violence and destruction. This violence was directed against Suharto and his family, against the rich generally, and against the Chinese in particular, who though only 4% of the population controlled most of the businesses. Jakarta today is an angry and traumatized place and will not be quickly rebuilt.

The Big Durian squats on the coast of Java, an awesome challenge for the Christian Church, a flavour perhaps of the 21st century. How will the Church respond?

– 2 –
Beliefs

You can make two statements about Indonesia's majority faith and both of them are true.

1 Indonesia is home to the largest Muslim community in the world.

2 Indonesia is *not* a Muslim country.

You are aware that this is not your standard Muslim country as soon as you get seated on the Sempati Air plane. While the Boeing rumbles around the tarmac, you might notice an *Invocation Card* tucked next to the flight magazine in front of you. A sort of divine safety leaflet, it suggests prayers for believers from each of Indonesia's recognized faiths – the Muslims, Buddhists, Hindus, 'Katoliks', and 'Protestans'.

Snug in your modern Sempati Air seat, you might not feel the need for urgent intercession. But the cards are well-thumbed.

Protestants are encouraged to pray the first seven verses of Psalm 108. ('Your faithfulness reaches to the skies.') The Catholic prayer roams the Bible in search of the appropriate metaphor:

> *Long ago you saved the children of Israel who crossed the sea with dry feet . . .*
> *We beg You, bless us with a safe trip, with good weather. Bless us with the guidance of your angels . . .*

The Islamic prayer is pragmatic:

> *. . . Oh Allah, shower us with Your blessings and protect us on this journey from any hardship or danger and protect also our family and our wealth.*

ONE TRUE GOD, NEVER MIND THE DETAILS

Indonesia's unique and attractive religious laws were invented, or even, as some have claimed, 'unearthed' by the first post-colonial President, Sukarno.[1] They offer perhaps the most imaginative of all Asia's attempts at getting religious communities to co-exist. And you can't understand Indonesia without them.

The principle written into Indonesia's national ideology, *Panca-Sila*, is simple. The state endorses faith in God, as expressed in the major religions. Every Indonesian has to belong to one of the five prescribed faiths. And the faiths have to coexist peacefully. Indonesia – and this is deeply held – is a religious country, not an Islamic one.

By law, everyone – everyone the Government has reached, that is, not counting the tens of thousands who still cut their way through the rainforests, innocent of what awaits them – must be a Muslim, a Protestant Christian, a Catholic Christian, a Hindu, or a Buddhist. Tough luck if you follow Chinese religions or are atheistic or agnostic or New Age or if you worship rocks. Or even if you are in the middle of some dark night of the soul and don't what you are. No matter. One of the five leading religious global brands has to go on your ID card, your *KTP*.

This has consequences:

- It is unthinkable, indeed it is risky in Indonesia to have no religion. Part of the Panca-Sila idea is to exclude atheists, who are understood to be communists, and who are still popular bogeymen[2] in these parts. In Indonesia, you are as sure about your religion as you are about your gender. (Possibly more so.)

- It follows that words like 'Muslim' and 'Christian' and 'Buddhist' are none too reliable as pointers to what a person is really all about. Of course, many who are badged as Christians or Muslims or whatever would be recognizable by fellow believers as the real thing. But many others, bearing the same labels, would not.

BENEATH THE SURFACE

Dispense with the labels, however, plunge into what people really believe, and you find another, exotic, spiritual world.

Many peoples have settled on the Rim of Fire over the centuries: first, animists; then Hindus and Buddhists; then Assyrian Christians[3]; then Muslims (initially Sufi Muslims, the mystics); and finally the Europeans, who brought Catholicism, Protestantism, communism and materialism.

If you believe the *KTP* identifications, Muslims would be about 86% of the population, Christians perhaps 11%[4]. In truth, neither the Qu'ran nor Christ has made such a decisive impact. The earlier beliefs have the deeper roots. One Christian worker said this:

> *Hinduism, Islam, Christianity, materialism: all have swept through Indonesia and been absorbed like spices, adding piquancy to the sauce but not really changing the basic nature of the dish.*[5]

Another described the faith in one province, Maluku, as 'animism with a frosting of Christianity.' Abdurrahman Wahid, the soccer- and democracy-loving leader of a 30-million strong Muslim organization has claimed that real practicing Muslims in Indonesia form 'at most' 40 percent of the population.

Nor would you guess the official religious affiliations from the treasures in the National Museum in Jakarta. There you'll find Indian gods, Buddhas, spirit-masks, and a treasure trove of golden cups, daggers and knives. Indonesian Islam has created little great art: nor has the Christian faith; magic and mysticism have.

MAGIC AND MYSTICISM

If Indonesians can be generalized at all, it wouldn't be as Muslims or Christians or the rest, but as mystics: spiritually aware, superstitious, surfers of the suprarational superhighways:

- In 1994 the Indonesian government toyed with the idea of making it a crime to offer to harm someone through sorcery.[6]

- Organizers claimed a Muslim rally in Jakarta was in no danger of running out of control, because 2,500 jinns were acting as spiritual policemen.[7]

- A Christian worker wrote:

    On the southern coast of West Java lies the very quiet town of Pelabuan Ratu (The Queen's Port). The people of Pelabuan Ratu, like most of the population of West Java, hold very strongly to their animistic beliefs, although almost all of them are professing Muslims. In fact, the 4 star hotel at the beach has a room permanently reserved for the Goddess of the Sea, Dewi Nyai Roro Kidul. The staff of the hotel claim that she stayed there last year.

- Every village in Bali (Indonesia's largely Hindu province) has a temple; virtually every house contains a shrine to local gods. Tourist promotion literature boasts: '[the Balinese] have devised a vast repertoire of exorcistic dances to drive the evil spirits away.'

- At some Christian churches in Halmahera, worshippers will sacrifice a chicken and pour its blood around the building before the service begins.

- The island of Timor has become well-known because of the 100,000 or so who died after Indonesia annexed the Eastern part of it in 1976. (This move is still considered illegal by the United Nations.) Less well-known is the deeply occult nature of its Catholicism and Protestantism.

  One (Protestant) researcher: 'The Timorese consider the environment is controlled by spirits . . . The sorcerers in each village can predict the future, and ensure good relations between the villagers and the spirits . . . Catholic priests in rural areas have been attributed sacred powers by the animists. Catholicism has influenced the ruling and urban classes most who nevertheless continue pagan practices.'

- The Bataks of Sumatra, Lutherans, are one of the world's great Protestant peoples. Yet Batak graves are sometimes sited in the middle of a rice field. The grave-marker (a house or a church) will have a cross on top; one reason for siting the grave there is the belief that departed spirits linger and may help boost the crops. Some Bataks will go to the *dukun*, the spirit healer, for cures. A child may be baptized wearing good-luck charms.

- In north-west Sumatra, the Acehnese people are perhaps the most strictly orthodox Muslims in all Indonesia; Aceh province has been called 'the doorstep of Mecca.' Yet even there observers report:

  Islam is strong [among the Acehnese] but exists alongside an 'heretical, pantheistic mysticism'; magic is significant in agricultural practice; interpretation of dreams is widespread and sickness is attributed to evil spirits and cured by magic.

THE DREAM-TIME INFOBAHN

Central to Indonesian mysticism are dreams. Magazines run pages of advice from dream agony aunts, explaining the niceties of interpretation. Dreams are taken seriously and sometimes contain important information.

This (to the West) bizarre communications highway sometimes carries Christian messages too and has helped spread God's kingdom in Indonesia. Two stories of people who subsequently became well-established Christians:

One girl had a dream and asked her Muslim friends to interpret it. They couldn't, so she asked a Western Christian worker whom she knew. This was the dream:

> I was standing in front of a wall, and the other side of the wall was a lovely garden – indescribably lovely. I tried climbing the wall, but it was too high. Then I tried walking around the wall, first one way, then the other. Finally I came to an iron gate, but it was padlocked. I picked up a twig and tried to spring the padlock, but I couldn't. I started to cry.
>
> Suddenly, a man in white touched me on the shoulder. 'Trust me', he said. 'I'll take you through the gate.'

She asked the missionary, 'Do you know who the man in white was?'

A faithful village evangelist, who had asked God for years for a wife, suddenly announced to a Western friend, 'I'm going to get married!'

'Wonderful!' he replied. 'Who is she?'

'Oh, I haven't met her yet,' the evangelist replied. 'But I had a dream about her.'

In his dream, the evangelist had seen a bird alight on his shoulder (which he understood as a symbol of marriage). He then followed the bird as it fluttered through a part of the jungle he didn't know, until it stopped at a house in a clearing.

Two weeks later this evangelist, on a trip, found himself in the part of the bush he had dreamt about. Remembering the way from his dream, he walked through the jungle until he found the clearing and the house. He knocked on the door and asked the head of the household, a Muslim,

'Do you have any daughters?'

'Yes, I have one.'

He explained the dream and asked for permission to marry the man's daughter (a girl whom he had not yet even met).

'Yes,' replied the father. 'Would you like to meet her?'

'Yes.'

The girl was brought, and the evangelist told her the dream and asked her to marry him.

'Yes,' she replied.

'But you'll have to become a Christian,' added the evangelist.

'OK.'

. . . and she did.

What another scholar wrote concerning the Sundanese of West Java (who, with a population of 30 m are the largest unreached people in the world), could be true of all: 'Islam dictates how [the Sundanese] act, not what they believe: the face of the monolith is Islam but the mind and heart is the Sundanese *adat* [tribal custom].'

A SPIRITUAL LAND

So:

- On the surface, and officially, and for formal occasions, Indonesia is carved up neatly between the five leading religious global brands, with Islam having the dominant share.

- At heart the real faith of many in Indonesia is a folk spirituality, tolerant, dreamy, magical, and only tenuously related to the official beliefs.

– 3 –
How the Church happened

The 11% or so of Indonesians who are badged 'Christians' are, we can guess, a mixed bunch.

- The Christian faith of some people is apparently little more than a cultural icon, something their tribal grouping has embraced. Mysticism is their living religious reality.

- Others, in contrast, have experienced first-hand the powerful working of God, believed in Jesus Christ, and made a decisive break with the occult.

- And many are somewhere in between: gazing at the sunlit theological peaks, dwelling in the mystic valleys.

Where did all of this Christian activity come from? How did the Church happen?

A HISTORY OF MISSIONS IN FOUR-AND-A-HALF PARAGRAPHS

The way Christianity developed in Indonesia reads like a compact history of Christianity in the non-Western world. You can summarize it under just four heads: Assyrian Christians; Catholic colonizers; Protestant colonizers; independence and further growth.

Arab sources tell us that Assyrian Christians could be found on Java and Sumatra from as early as 645 AD;[1] these are the same ardent missionary types who ranged from Syria all over Asia while Europe was enjoying its 'Dark Ages'.

The Assyrian Christians played for the losing side in the first-millennium theological battles that shaped Christian orthodoxy.[2] The Assyrian Church spread widely and flowered rapidly, was cut down by the Mongol invasions of Asia, and never recovered. Having bloomed in China, India, and Indonesia, it vanished from them all.

Much later came the Europeans, for whom the 'East Indies' meant the 'Spice Islands' and fabulous opportunities to make a fast *escudo* or *guilder*. The Portuguese (and hence Catholicism) came first (1500 or so); the Dutch (who were Protestants) took over (1600 or so); and apart from a hiccup in the early 1800s, Dutch rule in various forms continued until the Japanese invasion during the Second World War.

Christianity came along with the colonists, though it was not until the early nineteenth century that the first full-time Protestant missionaries got going. Since then the Church has done nothing but grow.

NINETEENTH CENTURY: PEOPLE MOVEMENTS

The Dutch were reluctant to let missionaries work among the many tribes and regions of Indonesia that were already Muslim. The missionaries had to concentrate on the animists.

These pioneers saw spectacular movements to Christ and you could fill many a Victorian biography with their daring deeds. The brilliant Ludwig Ingwer Nommensen came to Batakland – north Sumatra – in 1862, in danger of becoming a dessert: two previous missionaries to the area had ended their careers in a cooking pot.[3]

Undeterred – and typical of his age – he foresaw a day when:

> Where stand now only uncultivated hills, I see fair gardens and flourishing woods, and countless well-ordered villages of Christians. I see Batak teachers and pastors standing at the desk and in the pulpit to teach and to preach.

He lived to see his vision come true. Nommensen found that, when the leaders of a longhouse converted, the rest of the tribe would often follow: 52 Batak Christians in 1866, for example, became 103,000 in 1911.[4] This was a pattern repeated on other islands: Sulawesi, Halmahera, Ambon. The global population of Lutherans and other flavours of Reformed Christianity was greatly boosted by these nineteenth century people-movements.

TWENTIETH CENTURY: HOW THE CHURCH GOT ESTABLISHED

The Indonesian church spent most of the twentieth century becoming indigenized and indispensable. In the period from independence right up to the current 'interesting times', Christians played a notable part in nation-building.

The two greatest convulsions in Indonesia's recent history until the present days were:

- The struggle for independence at the end of the Second World War

- The failed Communist coup in 1965 that brought Suharto to power.

Indonesian Christians shone as forces for good in both these trials.

In the independence struggles (up to 1949), Christians died alongside other Indonesians fighting the Dutch, and buried for ever the idea that the Church was a colonial religion that would depart with the colonizers.

In 1965 an attempted Communist coup[5] followed years of hyperinflation and poverty. Suharto, at that time an army general, led the forces that defeated the coup plotters. In the anarchic few months that followed, it has been estimated that between 300,000 and 400,000 alleged Communists were slain on the streets in Java and Bali. Indonesian citizens were the main killers. The Christians emerged from the chaos with a better reputation than other groups. Some sheltered people in danger and saved many lives.

TWENTIETH CENTURY: GROWING FAST

The twentieth century also saw the church growing fast, especially in the years following the failed coup. 1.1% of Indonesians were Protestant in 1900; this had become 6.0% in 1990, the last date for which we have official statistics.

Many people who had been sympathetic to aspects of Communism – for example its care for the poor – chose to follow Christianity. So did many who lost friends or relatives in the massacres or who were sheltered by the Christians.

At the same time – starting in West Timor somewhat before the attempted coup – was the 'Indonesian revival', a season when spiritual realities were experienced with unusual clarity and power.

It was real, though it never covered the whole of Indonesia. Many people, especially in the province of West Timor, had such a vital encounter with God that their ministries today still bear the stamp of it. Nominal, syncretistic churches were transformed in dramatic seasons of repentance. Some who were touched by the revival served God all over the archipelago, strengthening churches.

Here's the testimony of one leader from Java who also experienced revival at that time:

> In 1967 our Bible College experienced the visitation of the Holy Spirit. For two whole months academic work came to a standstill. Classes were cancelled as the whole student body prayed together with the staff and we experienced the convicting power of the Holy Spirit and his cleansing from sin and from occult bondages. The Holy Spirit then mightily anointed the teams going forth throughout all of Indonesia, from Sabang, North Sumatra, in the western part of Indonesia, to the Moluccas in the eastern part, and from Sangir Talaud, in the northern part, to Timor, in the southern part. The Gospel teams, consisting of two, three or five members each, one hundred in total (both staff and students), were used by the Lord to bring the fire of the Holy Spirit everywhere they went.[6]

However, the revival and especially its miraculous bits was hyped in the West, at a time when Western Christians were themselves juggling with the charismatic movement and the Jesus movement. According to many observers, the planeloads of Western sightseers and the accompanying money and publicity hampered a notable move of God.

What is left of the revival today is many transformed lives; and the fact that some of the places where things happened are considered *kramat*, holy sites of interest to mystics.

Most of Indonesia's Christians and churches missed the revival altogether. But they still grew, a testimony at least in part to the power of the gospel and the faithful witness of Christians throughout the archipelago.

THE PORK FACTOR

Church numbers (especially in Kalimantan) also swelled because pork is unclean in Islam but not in Christianity.

After 1965, *Panca-Sila* was enforced with zeal. Everyone had to have one of the Big Five religions. Persuading some of Indonesia's animist tribes to forsake pig-keeping for the faith was like asking Americans to give up their cars for the Lord Jesus; it was not a strategy for growth. Animists were queuing up to have

'Christian' put on their *KTP* – regardless of whether they believed any of it (apart from the bits about pork).

OTHER FACTORS

Still other factors caused the churches to fill.

- *Education:* For most of the time that Indonesia has been a republic, the Christians have had the best schools. Many outside the faith have sent their children to them; and lost them to Christianity.

- *Image:* The Church has had the image (so unlike that in the West) of being somehow the modern, prudent, thinking person's choice of faith: better than the animism of the jungle or the Islam of the village.

- *Marriage:* Laws promoting religious harmony in Indonesia seek to ensure that people marry within their faith community. In practice – because almost any marriage is better than no marriage in many Indonesian cultures – lots of people convert to get married. Christians have become Muslims, and Muslims have become Christians. There have even been cases like one of a Muslim marrying a Hindu and both of them becoming Christians.

RARE YEARS

Perhaps it's no surprise that Church leaders report that the few years after 1965 were rare years of extraordinary openness to the gospel.

Foreign missionaries, too, saw a huge response. One missionary team, for example, systematically evangelized an area of Java containing three-and-a-half million people between 1966 and 1970, planting churches throughout the area. Every Sunday people were responding to the gospel. It wasn't that unusual to walk into a village, preach the gospel message, hand out leaflets, and establish a church in a single visit. The missionaries ran training courses, one week long, for new converts; some of these 'graduates' themselves then started new churches.

Another small team of missionaries, trekking far and wide through the chirruping rainforest of central Kalimantan, saw seven-and-a-half thousand animists enter Christianity in three years, in the face of fierce occult opposition.

Describing the way modernity (and especially the flirtation with Communism) had shattered their traditional beliefs the tribal folks said, 'Our longhouse has been destroyed and we're out in the bush and we need teaching.' Evangelists fresh from West Timor followed up and consolidated the work; nevertheless, starved of permanent pastors and teachers, and in many cases having failed to break with its occult past, the church remains mostly nominal today.

Such stories can be multiplied across the archipelago.

IN A NUTSHELL

And so the Church in Indonesia is:

- A product of prayer, preaching, sacrifice and revival

- A badge of convenience for lovers of roast pork

- And everything in between.

It's also big: as many as two million people may have signed up between 1965 and 1970 and high growth rates persisted into the 1990s.

WORK AMONG RESISTANT AND RESPONSIVE PEOPLE IN IRIAN JAYA

The following story appeared in Alliance Life (the magazine of the Christian & Missionary Alliance[7]), written by Edward Maxey, veteran missionary to tribal people in the rainforests of Irian Jaya.

There's no such thing as a typical missionary story from Indonesia. Turnings to Christ have happened amongst the poorest and remotest of peoples (as here) as well as among the richer (for example among the Chinese people of Bandung, who are now more than 50% Christian.) But similar stories to this can be told from many parts of Indonesia over the last 150 years.

This story began in dust and death 30 years ago. My wife and I were relatively young missionaries, working in the interior of Irian Jaya, Indonesia, and we saw God begin to move in a remarkable way. People throughout the Silimo region of Irian Jaya began to turn to the Lord. Whole villages burned their fetishes and put away their fear of evil spirits.

In those days we had demon possessed people around our house every day. When the spirits manifested themselves in men, these men fell on the ground and writhed and foamed at the mouth. Sometimes they grabbed a weapon and tried to kill or wound bystanders. However these evil demonstrations began to pass away, and the area increasingly was filled with singing and rejoicing as people came to know Jesus Christ.

Some resisted

There was, however, one sour note among the songs that began to echo across the Silimo region. Some old men who did not want to break with the past resented the freedom of the new believers. There were a few such people who resisted the gospel in most villages. Generally these were men who had been leaders in warfare and somewhat better off than their fellow villagers because they had received payments for services in black magic. These men grumbled and walked out of village meetings because a number of others were turning to Jesus Christ.

At one point their resistance turned to violence. Wawa was an evangelist from the lower Sinak Valley who came to Silimo to assist the work of the Lord there. He and his wife and one-year-old baby went to Walgaruk to witness and to found a church in that village. People there heard the gospel, prayed to receive Christ and burned their fetishes. However, some of those who resisted the gospel brutally killed Wawa's wife and child. They hacked him to death with axes and mutilated their faces.

Shortly after the murders the leaders among those who resisted the gospel left that area. They established new villages on the other side of the mountain in a valley called Mumnoak. Mumnoak became a valley of seven villages that were founded on the principle that the people who lived there did not want to know Christ.

In the meantime, life flourished for the people on the Silimo side of the mountain. More people became Christians. Gardens grew, sickness and sin diminished and 30 churches were established. People learned to read, clinics and schools were built and life improved in many ways.

Access by helicopter

We attempted from time to time to share the gospel with the people in Mumnoak. Several years ago, Mission Aviation Fellowship introduced a helicopter service into our area, and I asked the helicopter pilot to land in one of the villages of this valley. At that time I only left a gift of a sack of salt, thinking that, having demonstrated this concern for them, I would be able to come back in a few days to treat the sick and to witness concerning Christ.

However, three days later men from Mumnoak brought the sack of salt over mountain trails to our home with the word that they did not want any gifts from us. They also said if the helicopter brought me back again they would chop it up with their axes.

We let a few years go by, and then I decided to try to reach out to the Mumnoak again. My wife, Shirley, and I walked from our house in Silimo into their area.

Word of our arrival in the valley evidently preceded us, and when we came into one of the villages all the men were gathered together. No women or children were anywhere to be seen. I told the men why we had come and presented an ax head as a gift. I explained to them that we only intended to do good among them. I showed them that I had brought medicine to help them. Then I told them that I wanted to sleep in the village that night and talk to them about Christ the next day.

There was no discussion. The chief men pushed the ax back across the ground to me and said they did not want any of my things nor did they want medicine. They also told us they would not let us sleep in the area nor would they give potatoes to feed those who had come with us.

Sadly, we were forced to turn around and make our way back across the trails that we had travelled, struggling through the darkness to reach a village that contained Christians.

That trip took place 15 years ago. Since that unsuccessful effort we have sent messages to the people in Mumnoak from time to time. Once, when we heard that many there were dying from an influenza epidemic, we offered to bring them medicine. Again, however, we were spurned.

First words of hope

In April of this year the first words of hope concerning this area came to us. The people of Mumnoak sent us a message saying they wanted to receive gospel messengers. Pastors from Silimo went to the area to preach and returned to report that two villages on the other side of the mountain were willing to have evangelists live among them. 'We want to receive Christ before Maxey leaves Irian,' they said.

Churches in Silimo have sent two workers, Pinus and Hanus, to preach there. Up to 3,000 people have gathered to hear them preach, and the people have listened seriously to the gospel. Permanent houses are being built for evangelists. We are praying for many of these people to come to Christ.

Spiritual work is not easy anywhere. Our experience with Mumnoak has taught us that it may take 30 years before the harvest begins to come in. However, if we are faithful to pray and to work, even a resistant area can eventually be reached for Christ.

– 4 –
The far side: where the gospel isn't

ACROSS THE STRAIT

From Surabaya, the sprawling, humid capital of East Java, you can take a crowded ferry to the island of Madura.

Madura is easily visible from Surabaya. All that separates them are a few miles of browny-green strait garnished with Indonesian navy ships, sail boats, rusty cargo vessels and perhaps a cruise liner bobbing, gleaming white, in Surabaya harbour.

Surabaya has hundreds of churches. Some of them have thousands of members. Madura Island, with about the same population, and near enough for the government to plan a bridge crossing, has rejected Christian testimony for nearly a century and a half. Time and again the gospel has flickered into life in a community, and then been snuffed out.

A WORLD APART

Disembarking the ferry at Bangkalan, Madura, you may notice a certain pushiness in the air. Minibus drivers recruit energetically for passengers. If you stand out because of your skin colour, you find beggars tugging at your arms and body ('Hello! Hello!'). In the market a crowd blocks your path, smiling, asking questions, a stockade of people.

Stallholders are eager. On offer, beside the heaps of lovely fruit and sweets, are tourist trinkets: fake bullwhips; sickle-shaped knives, assorted sizes, with woolly handles for a good grip.

Madura island feels like a place apart from Java: poorer, more rural, more Islamic. You're more likely to see a pony-and-trap than the smoked-glass 4x4s in which the urbanized rich of Java cruise.

You aren't surprised to learn that this is the homeland of quite a different people from the Javanese. Unlike the Javanese, the Madurese are not famous for their gracious ways:

> The Madurese have a reputation for being rough, hot-headed and easily offended [wrote one observer]. Some have characterized them as ruthless and violent. These descriptions are not without some basis but should not be used as general characterizations. The custom of corak, avenging one's honor or some wrong by sneaking up on someone and cutting their throat or disembowelling them with a sickle-shaped knife, has provided the Madurese with this violent reputation. The custom is reality and still occurs yet is on the decline.

Well that's all right then.

Indonesia's third largest ethnic group, the Madurese are said to consider themselves *santri* or pure Muslims, compared with the *abangan*, compromised Javanese. Javanese may become Christians (perhaps 8% of them have); Madurese do not. One seasoned observer noted:

- 99.9% of Indonesian Christians do not believe the Madurese can become Christians

and

- 99.9% of Madurese are of the same opinion!

THE CHURCH: FOUNDERING, NOT FOUNDED

It hasn't been for lack of effort or love. Invisible barriers, spiritual and cultural, have kept the gospel out in nearly a century and a half of trying.

For example, it has taken more than a century to get a Bible to the Madurese, a history littered with untimely deaths, misunderstandings, and forgotten or lost manuscripts. Here are some of the highlights:[1]

1861: Arrival of Samuel Harthoon of the Netherlands Missionary Society.

1868: A band of Madurese, with the consent of local leaders, break into Harthoon's house and kill his wife; Harthoon leaves.

1880–1886 Dr Julius Peter Esser, another Dutchman, translates the New Testament. Takes it home to Holland. Runs into problems trying to publish it.

1889 Esser dies, aged 37. H van der Spiegel arrives in Madura, learns Madurese, revises Esser's unpublished translation.

1890 Esser's gospels and Acts published.

1912 van der Spiegel's complete revised New Testament, handwritten in 24 exercise books, is ready for publication. Luke and Mark are published, along with a compilation of 104 Bible stories.

1919 van der Spiegel dies. His (still unpublished) New Testament collects dust for several decades.

1933 F Shelfhorst, who has worked among the Madurese since 1904, produces a beautifully presented edition of the Psalms in Madurese. Works on translating the epistles; stencilled copies are distributed on Madura.

1939–1945 During the Japanese occupation of Indonesia, Shelfhorst is interned along with another expatriate and old friend, A J Swanborne. Together they retranslate the whole New Testament into Madurese.

1945 Shelfhorst and Swanborne die only weeks before the end of the war. Their precious New Testament manuscript is passed on to the Netherlands Bible Society in Bandung. And apparently lost.

1994 The 12m Madurese finally get a printed Bible in their own language, 108 years after a first draft was completed.

Evangelistic efforts among the Madurese people have suffered a similar fate. People profess faith and then turn back. Small congregations are established, then broken up or sent into terminal decline.

Near the culmination of his brilliant missionary career, in 1935, F Shelfhorst baptized 100 Madurese, which is probably a record. In the 1960s an Indonesian pastor built up a congregation of 50 or so. Other groups have started over the years. Few if any have taken root and grown.

A steady trickle of people, both pure Madurese and people who are half Madurese and half something else (Javanese or Chinese for example) are joining Indonesian churches on the mainland. But what David Bentley-Taylor, historian of Indonesian church growth, wrote in 1967 remains true today: 'Every effort to found a satisfactory and expanding Madurese church fell just short of success.'[2]

THE FAR SIDE

Indonesia contains many similar peoples, usually smaller in number than the Madurese, but equally lacking in an indigenous Christian presence. People who count these things have totalled up 130 ethnic groups within Indonesia that have a population of 10,000 people or more and that are 1% Christian or less. One hundred and twenty million people belong to these ethnic groups.[3]

Include also the smaller ethnic groups (those with fewer than 10,000 members), and the groups that are between 1% and 5% Christian, and you see that God's wish-list is long. The detail and complexity is awesome. For example, even the relatively Christian Maluku province has a definite need for New Testaments to be translated into 40 local languages, on top of the 23 languages already being worked on.[4]

Together these peoples make up a segment of Indonesia that is like the far side of the moon as far as the gospel is concerned: its back is always turned to us.

These unreached peoples are found in Sumatra (on the northern tip and the southern half); in West Java, where the Sundanese live; on the coastal fringes of the other islands where you can find groups like the Bugis, the Gorontalo, and others; and in the tribal interiors. Most peoples are Muslim, a number are animist, one or two Hindu.

Protestant Christians have made attempts to start churches among some of these peoples, as with the Madurese. In many other cases – for example among two dozen or so ethnic groups in South Sumatra – it seems that hardly anyone has tried at all.

What are the prospects for these peoples? We need to note several points.

TREADING CAREFULLY

It's hard to think of anything that would more upset the neighbours, and trouble the government, and endanger national security, and cause violence, and restrict visas for foreigners, than bold, public, plans for evangelizing Indonesia's unreached peoples. Indonesian Christian leaders shudder at the thought. Headline-grabbing schemes in this country are not kind, not wise, and not necessary.

One problem is that any discussions of evangelization in Indonesia would be understood (reasonably enough) by Muslims in Muslim terms. Christians may be talking of making available a message of personal transformation; Muslims would be hearing 'Christianization', the legal enforcing of Christian belief on a society. That's hard to swallow, especially when Muslim memories of 'Christian advance' are informed by accounts of 'Christians' slaughtering their way through the East during the Crusades.

UNREALISTIC, TOO

Talk of discipling great swathes of these unreached peoples also happens to be unrealistic. On the whole, these peoples are more solidly Muslim than the rest of Indonesia. The Church has grown so far by welcoming people who were, at heart, animists, mystics or even Communist sympathizers. Real Muslims turning to Christ account for a minority of the conversions – causing, at most, a change of only a few percentage points in the relative size of the Christian and Muslim communities.

On this evidence we can assume that Indonesia will be a majority Muslim nation for the next century and beyond, whatever anyone does.

SALT AND YEAST

The more realistic prospect is that the gospel will infiltrate all these unreached peoples, but lightly. The model is salt or yeast – a little, here and there. This is already happening and will continue, for a number of reasons, for example:

- The church
- Development
- Bible distribution
- Media ministry

THE CHURCH

Unusually for a mostly Muslim country, Indonesia is home to a large, indigenous Protestant Church. Most churches use the national language and so are accessible to people of most ethnic groups.[5]

You can find churches wherever Christians have set up home throughout the archipelago, in almost every town. If you have two Bataks in a town you have a church, the saying goes; three, you have a choir; four, you have a church split (and thus two churches)!

Several congregations (Chinese or Javanese) function on Madura Island. Five churches worship God in the capital of Aceh province, home to the most famously zealous Muslims in all Indonesia. Several thousand people have turned up for Christian meetings in what are on paper some of the most starkly non-Christian areas of the nation, for example in South Sumatra. So there's Christian testimony throughout the islands.

It's true that many churches are rather inward looking. But (as we shall see in Chapter 6) some parts of the Church are stirring themselves on behalf of Indonesia's unreached ethnic groups.

DEVELOPMENT

Indonesia's industrialization also stirs the pot. People leaving rural villages to look for city jobs seem to feel freer to convert to Christ. The Minangkabau people of West Sumatra, for example, are almost all Muslims in their homeland; but there's a small Minangkabau Christian fellowship in Jakarta.

BIBLES

Bibles and portions of scripture are read carefully here in Indonesia, sometimes passing through four or five different pairs of hands. The widespread use of Indonesian means that a good majority of people can read the scriptures in a

---

WILD HOPE

Christian hope is such that people will try all kinds of foolhardy and madcap ventures if they believe God is with them. Such wild hope has animated several generations of missionaries – local and expatriate – to go to Indonesia's unreached peoples, despite the gloomy prospects.

Today there is no sign of the Madurese or any other of Indonesia's unreached peoples turning to Christ in large numbers. People's best efforts through several generations have yielded small and precarious gains (at best). If the missionaries among these peoples were the sales force for a multinational company, they and their product line would have been abandoned long ago.

But hope is stubborn stuff, and you can always find kindling for it. A snippet from a missionary magazine:[6]

> A friend was recently taken to three villages where there are small groups of Madurese believers. In one village three large crosses dominated the road coming into the village – with a blood-stained Jesus in the middle.
>
> We didn't realize there were such groups of believers, and certainly not ones that were so forward in their confession of their new faith. It makes us wonder how many more believers there are hidden away in the kingdom of God. It is without a doubt a result of the concentration of prayer for the Madurese over the past few years.

Here's another:

> In 1991 seven Madurese were prepared for baptism. Threatened with violence all but one backed off . . . The Indonesian pastor who baptized him said, 'Ten years ago my wife and I sold our wedding rings so we could follow the Lord's work and reach the Madurese people. This one soul is well worth our wedding rings.'

David Bentley-Taylor digs out a beautiful illustration that may help explain why some Christians, in hope, keep loving the Madurese and the tribes in Indonesia like them.

Near the town of Pamekasan and almost in the centre of Madura Island there burns on a hillside 'The Eternal Flame'. In the middle of a field lies a small fire, four feet square. Although there is no visible fuel, flames dance up from dry stones and sandy soil. This patch of ground has burnt continuously, wet or fine, for as long as anyone can remember.[7]

The hope Christians have is that Madura Island's Eternal Flame – odd and insignificant, yet strangely unquenchable – is a reminder of how God works sometimes, keeping a tiny fire burning. And they believe God for a greater day.

language they understand. And as we noted, translations into an increasing number of local languages are being published and distributed.

MEDIA MINISTRY

The national mass media, reflecting Indonesia's stance as a religious country, sometimes broadcasts Christian programmes. On Good Friday 1994 – to give just one example – the *Jesus* film was shown on national TV. Christians were swamped with questions from people of other faiths the next day.

Media ministries from overseas are also lightly dusting unreached areas with the gospel. Christian radio is broadcast in 15 languages across Indonesia.[8] The broadcasts are popular; often they are the only radio broadcasts in the people's native tongue. The Acehnese print the broadcast times of the Christian shows in their newspapers.

One radio station in the Philippines receives 30 to 50 responses per week for each minority-language programme – despite the fact that for some in the audience, mailing a letter overseas costs half a day's wage and a week's walk.

Other media approaches are also yielding results – or at least making an impact. The news magazine *Tempo* (shortly before it was closed down by Suharto for criticizing a government minister) published a letter warning Muslims that some Christian group was sending Bible Correspondence Courses into Indonesia. Indonesian pastors have privately described Bible Correspondence Courses from abroad as among the most effective ways of explaining the gospel in unreached parts of the nation.

CONCLUSION

To sum up: you can count well over a hundred peoples in Indonesia that are less than 1% Christian. This body of peoples is not completely immune to the gospel. But – unless God has some surprises up his sleeve, if we can so speak – they aren't likely to succumb to its power any time soon.

– 5 –
Interesting times

A QUICK REVIEW

Here's the story so far:

- Indonesia is the farthest east of all the Muslim world, and it shows. In this country spirituality, mysticism, tolerance, and flexibility set the agenda: Javanese values, rather than Islamist ones.

- The Christian church has thrived here: the Eastern church (that is the Assyrian Christians) had a foothold for perhaps eight centuries; the Western church (Catholic and Protestant) has had Indonesian members from the sixteenth century onward. But you need to add that the people with *Christian* on their ID card represent many shades of belief.

- Though Christians can be found all over the archipelago, you can count 130 or so peoples in Indonesia with very little home-grown Christian witness. Most of them are Islamic. Almost the only people responding to the gospel out of these groups are the ones who've already left – physically, moving to Jakarta or to a new island, or culturally, forsaking traditional ways for modern ones. The Christian Church has failed to penetrate the homelands and heartlands of these peoples.

TURBULENCE

This chapter looks at some of the prospects for the future.

Whatever else happens, the Church would seem to be in for a rough and difficult ride.

During most of the 32 years of the Suharto era, the Indonesian Church enjoyed good growth in a context of national stability, civil peace, and growing prosperity. The economic earthquake and Suharto's fall changed all that.

The primary aim at the moment is surviving and coming to terms with that upheaval. Indonesia as I write this is a land where people struggle to feed their families, where businesses built up over years have been destroyed in a few months, where the fight against poverty has been rolled back two decades.

Beyond this economic calamity other issues threaten to shake the Church. We mention three:

- Growing discontent and violence
- An Islamic renaissance
- The political tide turning towards Islam

GROWING DISCONTENT AND VIOLENCE

As the 1990s unfolded the greed of the Suharto children began to outweigh the undoubted good of the Suharto-inspired development in many people's eyes. Shortly before the currency collapse, the Suhartos were estimated to be the twelfth-richest family in the world. The children had a financial interest in over 250 Indonesian companies, essentially the entire industrial economy of the nation.

Stories of individual rapacity led to a slow-burning fuse of anger across Indonesian society. A company involved with one Suharto son won the sole right to supply motorcycle helmets in Indonesia; a few months later parliament passed a law making it compulsory to wear helmets. A Suharto grandson, was, until grandad stepped in, cooking up a scheme to force all Indonesian schoolchildren to wear one brand of shoes (his).

Well before Suharto fell, cautious voices were warning him of the danger ahead. The moderate Muslim leader Abdurrahman Wahid was talking openly of some people's 'yearning to upset the apple-cart' and of people becoming convinced of 'the futility of non-confrontational ways'.[1] The godly President of the Communion of Churches, Sularso Sopater, was reported to have warned Suharto

in a private audience of the dangers ahead – in vain. All across society, the gap between the rich and the poor was an aggravation.

Violence and death were multiplying. For example, in 1997 hundreds of Muslim Madurese who had been resettled on Kalimantan died violently at the hands of another ethnic group, the partly Christian Dayaks; the reason was the Madurese settlers were displacing the Dayaks in the economic food-chain.

The riots that precipitated Suharto's downfall and ended the lives of more than 1000 people in two bloody days in Jakarta in May 1998, were primarily economic. In a $250m spree, shopping malls were looted and burnt; their high-tech contents re-appeared in poor areas all over the city.

Anger against Suharto's fallen 'New Order'[2] and clamour for change are, as I write this, the dominant trends in Indonesia. Indonesians are truly shocked at the stories of greed and rapacity that the newspapers are now allowed to print. It is like the time after an earthquake, when the ground is still rumbling and jolting with aftershocks, and no-one knows if further temblors are on the way or not.

Most of the current clamour calls for the kind of political and economic change that will bring Indonesia to happier, calmer waters. But really, no-one knows what will happen.

AN ISLAMIC RENAISSANCE

Take a bus through Java and you can't help noticing new mosque domes everywhere, as if some celestial lorry had tipped out a shining harvest of onions.

You have to be quite deaf to miss the throaty, bluesy, call to prayer that rolls against the mountain-sides five times a day. *Allah Akhbaaaaaar*. In a remote area of Kalimantan you can see loads of girders being hauled along jungle roads: most likely they'll be for a mosque, not a bridge. The numbers of people making the pilgrimage to Mecca rise each year.[3]

Indonesian fashion designers are producing gorgeous, Islamically acceptable dresses for women and girls. Islamic schools and universities are growing in prestige. Indonesian Muslim scholars are training at the best universities in the world. Islamic groups have started a quality newspaper to compete with the two well-known Christian ones; they also have the best news-magazines.

You can buy Islamic magazines containing testimonies of former Christians and descriptions of how guitar-strumming Muslim teachers have started an Islamic Sunday School and turned many children to The Religion. Some magazines publish the names and addresses of former Christians who have returned to the

Muslim fold: one mosque might have 15 names, another, 90. All of these are signs of newly vital, confident, Islam that is appearing in Indonesia.

THE POLITICAL TIDE TURNS

This Islamic renaissance in turn attracts the politicians. A 1997 survey commented: 'Islam as a focus for protest is growing, not just among the urban and rural poor, but among some students and intellectuals as well. For them, religion offers an alternative both to the stifling restrictions of the New Order and to the slavish aping of Western models. It is quite a modern thing to be a practising Muslim.'[4]

Suharto's final years were characterized by attempts to attract and please the Islamic constituency. Politics in Indonesia, which traditionally treated all the Panca-Sila religions equally, began to take a 'greener' (more Islamic) hue in the early 1990s.

One of the ways that B J Habibie, Suharto's successor as President, accumulated political capital was by chairing an association of Muslim intellectuals through this time. Habibie may not himself be an Islamic firebrand. But it did his cause no harm to be seen to be championing Islam as political change loomed.

A strong temptation for all politicians in the coming chaotic years will be to make a pitch for the Islamic vote. Concessions to 'greenery' are likely to grow.

For example, the composition of the army, the cabinet, the civil service began to change through the 1990s, with Muslims replacing previous Christian incumbents. Some Muslims are even pressing for a quota system which would mean that the percentage of Muslims in these state institutions would reflect the population as a whole, rather than the individual abilities of the candidates.

It became a lot harder during the 1990s to get permission to build a church. One frustrated Indonesian Christian worker told me 'it takes 20 permissions and five years', a miasma of regulation that mosque-builders somehow avoided. Other churches had their licences revoked.

THE CHURCH ON A RIM OF FIRE

Upon these fault-lines, then, the Church sits, uncomfortably.

Consider these facts:

- Despite the erosion of the *Panca-Sila* principles that has already happened, you can still find Muslim commentators who claim Muslims are 'marginalized' in their country.[5] In the new, fomenting political world of post-Suharto Indonesia, these voices won't go away.

- Many of the Christians were rich. Perhaps 40% of the Chinese community – who are the mercantile heart of Indonesia – are Christians. In these days when the depth of cronyism and corruption is being highlighted within Indonesia, anger against the rich, and especially against the Chinese, has overflowed. Chinese women have been systematically raped.[6] Chinese properties have been looted and burnt. It will, according to one local observer 'take a very long time for the Indonesian Chinese to forget the carnage inflicted on them.'[7]

- Anti-Christian rhetoric and violence has increased alarmingly. You can hear anti-Christian rhetoric, often at bleary times in the early morning, broadcast from mosque loudspeakers; this is not in the spirit of *Panca-Sila*.

    Low-level violence had occurred for years, a church burnt here, a stone tossed into a prayer-meeting there. But the 1990s saw church-burning and anti-Christian riots accelerate dangerously. Between 1996 and 1998 almost 400 churches were burnt down. Several people lost their lives. Those 400 churches destroyed in the two years up to Suharto's downfall compared with perhaps 300 churches torched in the whole period from 1945 to 1995.

Nor is the violence simply anti-Chinese or anti-rich. Some of is purely anti-Christian, according to some Christian leaders in Indonesia: fuelled by extremist Muslims who gather together mobs to further their own Islamist ends.[8] One observer has talked of 'truckloads of Muslim activists with political motivation' driving hundreds of miles from Jakarta to take part in a church-burning.[9]

THE CHALLENGE

During Indonesia's previous two convulsions this century, Indonesia's Christians brought a lot of credit to the name of Christ. The challenge in this third period of instability is to do so again.

– 6 –
The challenge for the Church

HERE WE GO

How is the Church prepared for the turbulent times ahead?

The challenge for the Church is to provide a full-orbed, full-blooded response to Indonesia's current difficulties. The Church in this country does not have a choice between prayer, evangelism, frontier missions, demonstrating Christian integrity in society, works of compassion, nation-building, or working with other faiths for the national good. It has to do them all.

SEEING WHAT THE CHURCH IS MADE OF

You can crudely divide the Protestant Christians in Indonesia into two groups – the mainline churches and what I will call the 'Repentance churches'. Some of their characteristics could be put like this (if you forgive the stereotyping):

Type of church	Mainline	'Repentance'
Percentage of Christian community	80%	20%
How (most people) join	Born; baptized as a baby	Conversion experience; baptized as adult
Theological flavour	Reformed, Lutheran, Methodist.	Baptist, Pentecostal, Charismatic.
Worship style	Formal	Spontaneous
Leadership preference	Academically gifted	Spiritually gifted
Aim?	'Every person perfect in Christ'	'Make disciples of all the nations'
How to achieve stated aim?	'You can't organize the Holy Spirit': Love, salt, light	'You must strategize': Evangelism, spiritual warfare, suffering.
Criticisms of the other camp	Nominal. Syncretistic. Inward-looking. Lacking discernment in spiritual things.	Zealous without knowledge. Anti-intellectual. Lacking wisdom.

All this is an oversimplification:

- You find many 'repentance churches' that choose to affiliate with the mainline churches' national body, the Communion of Churches.

- You find strategic evangelistic vision and highly effective outreach in many of the mainline churches. For example, I know of a 'mainline' type congregation that is seeing 100 Sudanese a year coming to the Lord. In another, half its 1000 congregation are from a Muslim background. (They tend not to broadcast these facts in quite the way the repentance churches would.)

- Some streams of Protestantism don't fit in any of these schemes, for example the non-charismatic evangelical churches, who have seen thousands come to Christ and have a clear evangelistic vision, but who would definitely resent being badged as either 'charismatic' or 'mainline'.

Together this large collection of Christian people has many strengths.

THE 'REPENTANCE CHURCHES'

The approximately 20% of the Protestant camp that I have called 'repentance churches' are often ardently evangelistic. They are not afraid of people or demons. They are bold. Many of their exploits seem to come from the pages of *Acts*. You feel proud of them. A few examples:

How challenging [an expatriate Christian worker wrote] to hear a petite Bible school student share how through her prayers in the name of Jesus a demonized man was delivered after fifteen witch doctors had failed to set him free. In this same mountain village a good number of Muslims have been converted and these very poor villagers are making bricks and gathering lumber with which they soon hope to erect their own place of worship.

- A church in Singapore sponsors hundreds of Indonesian missionaries from the 'repentance churches' who join the resettlement communities to which many Indonesians have moved from overcrowded Java and Bali. These missionaries have a year of Bible training, a year to plant a church, and then the sponsorship stops. Through its support this remarkable Singaporean Pentecostal church – with about 600 members – has helped spawn hundreds of new Indonesian congregations.

One of the first batch of these missionaries saw five people including the Principal of the village school turn to Christ in her first month of ministry on one island. Shortly after, she was caught up in a cholera epidemic and died on the boat that was ferrying her to medical help. Before she died she said to her companions:

'Some people ask why we go to give our lives to the villages. What's the benefit? But I thank the Lord that five people came to Christ . . . My life is well spent.'[1]

- A number of Bible schools have a great zeal for evangelization. The Evangelical Theological Seminary of Indonesia in theory only lets its students graduate when they have started a new church of 30 or more members.[2] Hundreds of new churches have been founded, and existing small fellowships strengthened, since the seminary was founded in 1979.

The 'repentance churches' are also tooling up to send missionaries of their own around the world. The first few are already sent; despite the financial crisis, more will follow.

THE MAINLINE CHURCHES

The mainline churches in contrast are far more cautious about direct evangelism and outreach. Their focus (in line with government policy) is preaching the gospel within the churches and caring for the whole person. For the most part they don't count heads, develop evangelistic strategies, or do the kinds of things that the 'repentance churches' would call spiritual warfare: miracles, healings, deliverance from demonic power and so on.

But these are the ones, above all, with a grand vision of the national good. They see the need for nation-building. They recognize they may have a role together with Muslims in building a pluralist society. They are keen for the social fabric to be spun afresh so that Indonesia becomes a more just society. Theirs is at best a prophetic, holistic vision of a church within a nation.

The negatives within each type of church are best glossed over: apathy, fear, nominalism, syncretism, the health-and-wealth gospel, empire building, power struggles, immorality and the rest. Just like they are in the West, these are huge, horrible problems, and they cause grief to many within Indonesia.

THE CHURCH IN THE TURBULENCE

How has this wide and varied Church responded to these current turbulent times? The elements of a courageous Christian response can be seen:

- *Intercession:* During the final months of the Suharto reign, a local Christian leader wrote about a 'movement of prayer sweeping throughout the country. Many prayer groups in offices, churches, homes, participate in prayer and fasting for our nation.'[3]

- *Engagement (I):* Shortly before Suharto resigned, 318 church leaders added their voice to the many calling for him to go. Suharto's departure was, by previous Indonesian standards, a peaceful affair. Christians can at least claim a small part in the credit for that.

- *Engagement (II):* A small group of Christians reportedly visited President Habibie shortly after he became president, explaining the case for religious tolerance, assuring him of their prayers for the country, and actually praying in person for him before they left.

- *Acts of mercy:* It was reported from several cities around Indonesia that during the food shortages following Suharto's fall, churches were buying food and fuel in bulk, and selling them on at subsidized prices to their neighbours, both Christians and non-Christians.

- *Teaching faith:* The call to trust the Lord in the midst of these difficulties is being made clearly and often in churches across Indonesia.

- *Quietly getting on with the job:* In a conference in January 1997, Indonesian Christians from across the spectrum committed themselves to bringing culturally relevant witness to the gospel of Christ into every one of Indonesia's remaining unreached peoples. This was the first time this commitment has been made by a representative body of the churches in all Indonesian church history.

These small signs are an indication of what the Church in Indonesia is about. They will need all their resources and character for the challenges ahead. Some of the calls on the Church:

- *Helping construct a free nation.* One of the ironies of the political tilt to Islam in recent years is that it is not exactly what the majority of Indonesians want.

  We have shown how the dominant form of Indonesian Islam, the Islam of the Javanese people, is fundamentally easy-going and peace-loving.

  People may be open to calls for redressing the political balance in favour of Muslims, for a recovery of Islamic vitality, and for promoting Islam as a bulwark against corrosive Western ways. But the large majority of Indonesians do not want their country to be an Islamic state modelled on a Middle Eastern or even a Malaysian example. We shall see in the next chapter that nearby Malaysia is carving out a role as modern, Muslim state. Indonesians would rather build a country that was modern, religious, and tolerant. Unified, as their national motto has it, within diversity.

  Whether they get such a nation or not depends what happens when the dust settles after the implosion of Suharto's New Order.

  Many people are eager to take charge of Indonesia in this testing time for the country: the hard-line Muslims who began to operate parts of Indonesia's goverment machinery in Suharto's final years are among them. So – worse – are certain sinister members of the army who, many believe, were behind the ugly anti-Chinese and anti-Christian violence of recent years. It's vital for the Church to trust God and work with others to see a decent leadership and government in these trying days.

- *Helping rebuild the economy.* We have seen that many of the Chinese-Indonesians fled for their lives at the fall of Suharto. Chinese Christian women have been called 'triple-minority' citizens, victimized because their sex, ethnicity, and faith.

The Chinese took their money out with them, albeit in piles of worthless rupiah. They left behind many gaps. Food shortages multiplied because the shops were closed up and the supply chains broken. Without the Indonesian Chinese, the prospects for salvaging Indonesia's wrecked economy are bleak. It may be that God calls many of them to return, despite the risks, and help rebuild their nation.

- *Being salt and light.* In what is sadly recognized as one of the most corrupt countries on earth, the Christians must continue lovingly to demonstrate Christ. The President of the Communion of Churches has spoken of the vital need to 'live out the gospel in all walks of life'.

- *Finishing the job.* And in the midst of all the chaos, the Church has been given its best-ever chance to bring a knowledge of Christ to each of Indonesia's unreached peoples. This is not a 'Christianization' programme; it is an attempt simply to see Christ known and loved in all the peoples among whom he is not accurately known or loved at the present time.

Church interest in this task has grown hugely in the 1990s. Prayer has (or seems to have) multiplied. Structures and personnel are being put in place. For the first time it looks like it might actually happen: it's possible that every people in Indonesia will have a small church of their own before the third Christian millennium has gone much beyond its first decade. That's not the fulfillment of Christ's Great Commission. But it's not a bad step along the way.

FIERY TRIAL

What we have called 'interesting times' in this book might in New Testament language be called 'fiery trials'. In church history, such times and trials are also once-in-a-lifetime opportunities for changing the course of the nation.

What they are most definitely not are easy or peaceful times. We might like to pray along with the Indonesian church that God would continue to build it up and make it 'strong, firm and steadfast'.[4]

WHAT OUTSIDERS CAN DO

In this interconnected age, all the parts of the body of Christ can intimately affect the others. What can we do? Here are a few suggestions.

See to our own house

I was asking a senior Indonesian church leader about what Indonesia's mainline churches were doing to fulfill Christ's Great Commission to make disciples of all peoples. Before he answered in detail, he gently rebuked me: 'Where in the West has Christ's Great Commission ever been fulfilled?' In Europe you have had the gospel for two millennia, he was implying, and you still can't point to a single 'discipled nation'.

I learnt this from him: the behaviour of the Church in the so-called Christian lands affects the Church in the places where the Christians are a small minority. If we bring dishonour to Christ, sooner or later it washes over the Indonesian church. It really is true that there is one body of Christ, all of us, and 'if one part suffers, every part suffers with it; if one part is honoured, every part rejoices with it.'[5]

Prayer and partnership

We have opportunities to partner with Indonesia's Church in prayer. Some people or churches may want to specifically 'adopt' one or more unreached Indonesian peoples as a focus for their prayers. Out of the prayers, opportunities for service in various ways may arise. Some of the resources at the back of the book will help you into this.

– 7 –
Elsewhere on the Rim: the Philippines and Malaysia

Indonesia's riches dominate the human geography of the region. Members of the same broad family, however, can be found beyond Indonesia's islands. We mention two groups especially, both of which have a large population but a small church.

- The Muslims of the Philippines
- Malaysia's Malays

THE MUSLIMS OF THE PHILIPPINES

The most populous country in the region after Indonesia is the Philippines: like Indonesia, it is a huge archipelago; like Indonesia, most people belong to some official faith (in this case, Catholicism) but spiritism, magic, and mysticism are the real currency of spiritual life for most.

Many of the same themes recur: giddy incursions of materialism as loggers invade jungles, bulldozing both trees and cultures. There's rumbustious industrial development in the great cities; forest-dwellers (even occasionally cave-dwellers) on the small islands and in the remote interiors; urban slums as the harsh interface between them.

You find robust church growth all over the Philippine archipelago. The Philippines, indeed, leads the world as the best developed example of the DAWN (disciple a whole nation) strategy in which Christian denominations combine plans to provide a culturally relevant church for every local community in the land.

According to a report in 1996[1], the number of evangelical churches had grown by between 8% and 10% each year for the previous 22 years to a total of 29,000

churches. As many as 20% of the Philippine population may currently belong to, or adhere to (or least be passing through) these churches. Fittingly, the headquarters of the World Evangelical Fellowship are located in the Philippines.

Yet as in Indonesia, the diversity of the place is awesome. God evidently loves Filipino cultures: he has created so many. More than 150 languages are heard within the Philippines' 7,000 islands. So, stories of rapid church growth tell only one part of the story. Before every community, DAWN-style, has its own local church there are many more New Testaments to be slowly translated, many cultures humbly explored.

Among these unreached ethnic groups are the Philippines' Muslim peoples. Most of the Philippines' Muslims live on the huge southern island of Mindanao, in tribes such as the 900,000 Magindanao and the 500,000-strong Tausug.

Outnumbered and marginalized, the Muslims have cause to complain about their treatment at the hands of past 'Christian' rulers of the Philippines. They fought bitterly against two hundred years of Spanish colonial rule. In exchange, crusader-like, the Spaniards destroyed mosques and carried off Islamic leaders. Muslims still feel the pain.

Hence it is not surprising that a violent minority in Mindanao have been fighting for independence in a quarter century of conflict that has seen perhaps 50,000 people die violently. Among these casualties were young volunteers from the short-term mission Operation Mobilization, killed when a hand-grenade was lobbed into one of their open-air meetings.

The gospel, then, still gets a prickly response among the Muslims of Mindanao and the other southern islands. Of the Philippines' 5m or so people who belong to Muslim tribes, only a few hundred have turned to Christ.

MALAYSIA'S MALAYS

Malaysia contains its own large branch of the Malay-speaking Muslim world (smaller numbers also live in Singapore, Thailand and Brunei).

The political and religious flavour here is quite different from that in Indonesia or the Philippines. Malaysia's economy is much better constructed than Indonesia's. Nor does the gap between rich and poor feel so great. And the Malaysian government has responded to Islamic revival by becoming far more clearly pro-Islamic than is Indonesia's government, even though only slightly more than half of Malaysia's population are actually Muslims.

Freedom of religion is guaranteed in the

Malaysian constitution but it is curtailed in practice in certain Malaysian states. Laws and cultural pressures against conversion are great: recent government moves included setting up a centre to help turn Muslim apostates back to Islam.[2]

Indonesian Christian literature and Bibles, which would be perfectly understood by Malaysians, are banned because they employ words that Muslims use for God, and may thus – it is argued – offend.

As in every Islamic country, Malaysia experiences many tensions between Islamic moderates and Islamist extremists. For example, 'apostasy', even when it involves a private family matter like a Muslim girl falling in love with a Catholic man, has made the national news.[3] In one recent bizarre instance, the Prime Minister went on TV to argue against people who wanted him to pass laws that would lead to 'apostates' like this girl being hanged.

A still deeper obstacle is the fact that Malay families are in general warm, close-knit, and loving. It's hard to bring shame and pain to such families, even in the cause of following your conscience.

Few Malays in Malaysia have turned to Christ. A Muslim anti-apostasy organization claims that between 4,000 and 5,000 Malay Muslims renounced Islam between 1982 and 1998.[4] Even that figure seems an exaggeration compared with the estimates coming from the Christian sphere.

THE CHURCHES

Malaysia's Christians, who are mostly Chinese, Indian or from the tribal peoples on Malaysia's half of the island of Borneo, are being squeezed by these Islamic pressures. A joint council of Buddhists, Hindus, and Christians frequently petitions the government about perceived inequalities. The Muslims, they claim, can run school clubs for children, construct religious buildings, bury their dead and live out their faith in many ways more easily than people of other religions.

Yet the Malaysian church has lots of faith and vision and is probably the fastest growing religion in the country. Worshipping with them would be a tonic for many of us from the West. In places they are innovative, energetic, (as befits Malaysia's image as a young, dynamic country), and world-class (if we can talk that way) in areas like children's ministry and intercession. They, too, warrant our prayers and friendship.

NOTES

CHAPTER 1

1 Kalimantan is the Indonesia name for the island of Borneo (which Indonesia shares with Malaysia and Brunei). It shares Irian with Papua New Guinea, Irian Jaya being the name for Indonesian half.
2 Estimate by Dr Kartawinda of the National Biological Institute. In just one 1.6 ha plot in Kalimantan, this researcher counted 203 plant species. (Philip Hurst, *Rainforest Politics*, London: Zed books, 1990, p 5.)
3 Yates, S and Domico, T: *The Nature of Borneo*, New York: Facts on File 1992, p 6.
4 *Economist* survey, July 26th 1997, p 15.
5 Between July 1997 and February 1998.
6 *Asiaweek*, Oct 6th 1993, p 30.
7 The other six (all of whose populations will be around 10m people or more) are Cairo, Karachi, Tehran, Baghdad, Istanbul and Dhaka.
8 According to a well-placed leader in the evangelical wing of the Church in a personal interview, June 1995.
9 See *World Pulse*, July 3rd 1998, p 5.

CHAPTER 2

1 Admittedly with some help from his Christian friends, who persuaded him at the last minute to remove a clause that would have made non-Muslims into second-class citizens.
2 Or if you prefer, bogeypersons.

3 That is, the Assyrian Church of the East. Officially called The Holy Apostolic Catholic Assyrian Church of the East, or more familiarly, but wrongly, known as the Nestorian Church, it was the most extensive denomination in the world in the eleventh and twelfth centuries, when it spread over 250 dioceses across Asia with 12m adherents. Today, the Assyrian Church of the East numbers only 800,000 people, mostly in Iraq. The apostles Bartholomew and Thomas are named as its first patriarchs.
4 No-one knows the true figures. No official statistics for the size of religious communities have been published since 1990.
The official statistics are:

Year	Christians as a percentage of the population
1971	7.4%
1980	8.8%
1985	9.6%
1987	9.85%
1990	9.6%

Almost all the church leaders and Christian workers to whom I spoke believed that the Church was still growing. Those who were willing to guess at its 1995 size would usually put it somewhere between 11% and 14% of the population. Eleven percent of the population in 1995 was just under 22m people. Approximately two-thirds of these people were Protestants.

Note that if relative sizes of the religious communities continued to change at the same rapid rate as in the 1970s and 1980s, Indonesia will still be more than two-thirds Muslim a century from now.
5 Unpublished orientation material.
6 *Asiaweek*, March 23rd 1994, p 31.
7 *Asiaweek*, June 9th 1993, p 41.

CHAPTER 3

1 An ancient book written by Shaykh Abu Salih al-Armini mentioned Fansur (Pancur), near Barus, as having many churches. These Christians were called Nestorians by the same Arab source. The source for this is Ukur, F and Cooley F L, eds, *Toil and Struggle: National Report of the Total Survey of the Church in Indonesia*: Jakarta: LPS DGI, 1979. (In Indonesian: its title is *Jerih dan Juang: Laporan Nasional Survai Menyeluruh Gereja di Indonesia*). Another early document describes an Assyrian archbishopric for Dabagh [Sumatra and Java], Sin and Masin [China]; and an early Franciscan Bishop, Marignolli, visiting Palembang (in Sumatra) reported the existence of a community of Christians there. I'm indebted to Dr Iman Santoso for all of this information.
It also seems Assyrian Christians were still present in the Malay archipelago as late as the fifteenth century.
2 Assyrian Christians are Monophysites, rejecting the council of Chalcedon, in contrast to the Greek and Western Christians. (But in common with the Coptic church of Egypt.) In practice, politics and geography better explained their separation from the rest of Christendom.
3 See Stephen Neill, *A History of Christian Missions*, Harmondsworth, Middlesex, England: 1964, pp 348–351.
4 Neill, p 349.
5 According to the official version of events.
6 Petrus Octavianus, founder of the Indonesian Missionary Fellowship, in his article *Divine Resources for Frontier Missions* (found in Sookhdeo, P, *New Frontiers in Mission* (Exeter, UK: Paternoster Press, 1987) p 137).
7 November 24th 1993.

CHAPTER 4

1 See David Bentley-Taylor *The Weathercock's Reward* for the definitive history of the gospel among the Madurese.
2 Bentley-Taylor, p 112.
3 Figures provided for a national Indonesian missions consultation, August 1997.
4 1994 figures.
5 A Bible translator pointed out to me, however, that many people (especially those from smaller and more remote ethnic groups) do not speak any Indonesian. And for many more people, Indonesian is the trade and legal language, not the language of the heart. The need for Bible translations into local languages is still acute.
6 *Worldwide*, The organ of WEC International in Australia, January 1995.

7 Bentley-Taylor, p 117.
8 For the record: Indonesian, Javanese, Sundanese, Minangkabau, Acehnese, Sasak, Balinese, Toraja, Batak, Banjar, Gorontalo, Bugis, Makasarese, Madurese, Ogan.

CHAPTER 5
1 Quoted in *The Economist*, May 10th 1997, pp 73–74.
2 The 'New Order' was the name given to Suharto's rule.
3 From 50,000 in 1984 to 192,000 (the maximum allowed under the quota for Indonesian pilgrims) in 1995 (*Asiaweek*, Dec 15th 1995).
4 *Economist* survey, July 26th 1997, p 8.
5 One British Muslim current-affairs magazine spoke of Indonesian democracy as 'a marvel of political engineering designed mainly by CIA academics in order to keep the country's 90% Muslim majority on the margins of power.' (*Impact International* March 1998, p 8.)
6 Press reports quoted, for example, an NGO called the Humanity Volunteers Team in Indonesia which received more than 50 rape reports from five different cities from the two days of rioting prior to Suharto's departure. Witnesses claimed the rapes were pre-planned and carefully orchestrated. Five of the raped women were burned to death and three others committed suicide.
7 In private correspondence, July 1998.
8 See the report from the *Compass Direct* news agency, June 20th 1997. (Email: Compassdr@compuserve.com.)
9 Private correspondence, June 1997.

CHAPTER 6
1 For more information on Glad Tidings Church see my article in the Singaporean magazine *Impact*, Feb/March 1994.
2 In practice this is not entirely the case. But that is not to detract from the fact that this school and others like it (the SETIA and Doulos schools might be even more successful) try to produce graduates who can actually win people to Christ and then establish them in new congregations of Christians. This is so rare a priority in theological training schools around the world that it is worth highlighting.
3 In a document issued by the National Prayer Network for Indonesia, January or February 1998.
4 See 1 Peter 5:8–10.
5 1 Corinthians 12:26.

CHAPTER 7
1 By the Philippine Council of Evangelical Churches.
2 See the *IISIC Bulletin*, Feb–Mar 1996 and Feb–Mar 1997.
3 Such a case was a front-page story in the Malay daily *Utasan Malaysia* on January 20th 1998, for example.
4 According to *Berita NECF*, the organ of the National Evangelical Fellowship of Malaysia, Vol 10, No. 2, March/April 1998.

RESOURCES

NATION AND CULTURE

For descriptions of Indonesia as a country and its culture you could do worse than looking up the standard books for travellers such as:

Draine, Cathie and Barbara Hall
　Culture Shock! Indonesia Times Books International, Singapore 1986

Attempts to explain Indonesian culture to Western and other expatriates.

Lonely Planet
　Indonesia – a travel survival kit
　Lonely Planet, Australia 1992

The classic travel guide for the curious and impecunious – though missionaries serving in Indonesia get to places even more remote than Lonely Planet's backpackers seem to have trod.

You can find equivalent books for other countries on the Rim of Fire.

UNREACHED PEOPLES

To follow up on the work among the unreached peoples, try these web sites:

//www.ad2000.org
　This is the AD2000 and Beyond Movement's website. AD2000 seeks to

network Christian ministries together with the aim of 'A Church for every people, and the gospel for every person' by the end of 2000.

//www.christian-info.com/html
This is the site of the 'Christian Information Network' which seeks to be the 'prayer track' of AD2000.

//www.bethany-wpc.org/profiles/home.html
Here you can find profiles of the world's least-reached peoples, including those of the Malay World. As I write this you can download individual profiles for free, or purchase a printed copy of all of them.

//www.brigada.org
Describes itself as 'a system of conferences and forums that allow you to network with others who share common interests in sharing God's love with previously unreached cities and peoples around the world.' So you can keep up with news and discussion (admittedly of varying quality).

//www.missionnet.org
Here you can sign up for mailing lists related to news about missions or prayer requests.

NEWS OF THE CHURCH

For news of the Church on the Rim of Fire you could try these sources:

Compass Direct
This press agency produces excellent reporting on the church in difficult or persecuted settings worldwide – in-depth, first-hand, eye-opening stuff. To subscribe, contact compassdr@compuserve.com

The *Bulletin* of The Institute for the Study of Islam and Christianity
This is a widely read and well-informed source that covers Christian issues throughout the Islamic world. Address: St Andrew's Centre, St Andrew's Road, Plaistow, London, UK E13 8QD.
Phone: 44 171 473 0743
Fax: 44 171 511 4874.

World Pulse
Published by the Evangelism and Missions Information Service of the Billy Graham Center at Wheaton College, this is a bimonthly 8-page newspaper, mostly made up of missions-related world-news snippets. Address: PO Box 794, Wheaton, Ill 60189, USA.
Phone: 1-630-752-7158
Fax: 1-630-752-7155
Email: Pulsenews@aol.com

//www.religiontoday.com
Here you can find a (free) searchable archive of brief church-related news stories on many countries.

WORKING IN THE RIM OF FIRE

For working in the Rim of Fire, either in a 'nation-building' secular job or in theological teaching, mission agencies can supply you with information, job opportunities, advice and much else. You may find their addresses in such standard sources as national Christian handbooks or *Operation World*. Or ask around at your church.

Alternatively, you could contact your national evangelical missionary alliance.

PRAYING FOR THE RIM OF FIRE

For the Church: praise God for its faith and love. Ask God to establish it in every good work and in every act proceeding from its faith. Pray that all parts of the Church will be renewed according to the truth. Pray for love and unity.

✧ ✧ ✧

For the governments in the different countries of the Rim of Fire. For wise and good leadership in the face of ethnic and religious differences, and economic challenges. For social justice.

✧ ✧ ✧

For the many peoples within these countries: that Christ will become incarnate within each one through the gospel, and that these peoples will coexist in peace together.

✧ ✧ ✧

For the poor: that they will know the Good News of Jesus working in power in their communities.

✧ ✧ ✧

For Christian leaders: for knowledge and wisdom, for integrity, and for the power of the Holy Spirit at work through their lives.

✧ ✧ ✧

For the enemies of the gospel, that they will find the love of God in Christ.